A 3-minute forever book

EAT YOUR PEAS™

for Me

By Cheryl Karpen
Gently Spoken Communications

At the heart
of this little book
is a promise.

It's a promise from
me
to
myself
and it goes like this:

Whenever I feel
a little blue
or simply need a
pick-me-up,
I promise to read
every page of this book
to remind myself
how truly **amazing** I am.

Sometimes I can be too hard on myself.

I take the weight of the universe on my shoulders
and believe it is mine to carry alone.

Other times, I forget how much people love me.

And I am **very** loveable

So, in the interest of
wholehearted
down to earth
can't-take-that
joy
away from me feeling,
here are some things
I need to know, remember,
and never, ever doubt:

I am a
one-of-a-kind
original.

That makes me
priceless.

I'm also learning the importance of taking precious time for myself.

Everyday I have
the opportunity
to love more,
learn more,
and
experience more.

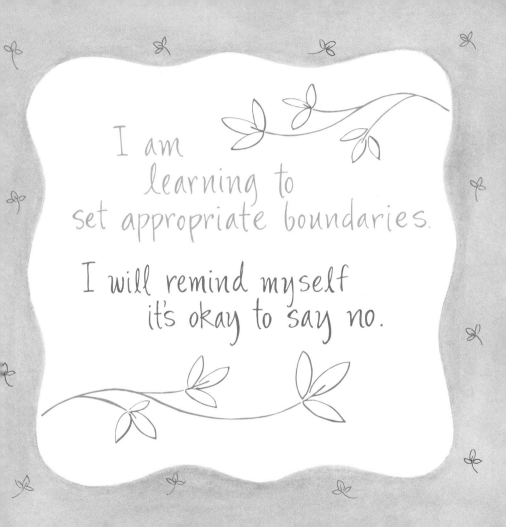

I am
learning to
set appropriate boundaries.

I will remind myself
it's okay to say no.

I used to think
people could
read my mind.
Now I'm learning
to
ask
for what I want.

I'm not going to waste
any more time
feeling sorry for myself.

There is simply too much
living to do.

Today is going to be
a good day!

I'm learning to
forgive myself
for being less than perfect.

(That goes for all the other
imperfect people
in my life, too.)

I've come to realize
I'll live a more
peaceful and happier life
if I don't impose
guilt, shame,
and impossible expectations
on myself and others.

Trying to control
others
is exhausting.

Trying to control
myself
is a big enough job!

When I become discouraged,
when my life
doesn't go as planned,
I will remember
there is a much greater plan for me.

I count my blessings every day.
I am grateful for:

_____

_____

_____

If anyone can,
I can !

I know that by
helping others
reach toward their dreams
I move that
much closer to
mine.

I want my life story
to be a real page-turner
filled with
discovery
and
purposeful living.

Each new sunrise
is a reminder that
every day is a new beginning.
I can't wait to see
what tomorrow holds for me.

I can hardly wait
to wake up each morning.

I get
kinder,
smarter,
brighter,
healthier,
and wiser
every day.

I am a very important somebody and no one — not one person — can take away my magnificence.

I am worthy of loving and being loved. I am worthy of being treated with respect.

I am an amazing individual with a wonderful heart and spirit.

I am enough.
I am enough.
Oh, yes, I am enough!

I will
take care of me,
love me,
cherish me,
honor me,
hug me.

And yes,
I will remember to

eat my peas!

Why Peas?

She was a vibrant, dazzling young woman with a promising future.
Yet, at sixteen, her world felt sad and hopeless.

I was living over 1800 miles away and wanted to let this very special young person in my life know I would be there for her across the miles and through the darkness. I wanted her to know she could call me any time, at any hour, and I would be there for her. And I wanted to give her a piece of my heart she could take with her anywhere—a reminder she was loved. Really loved.

Her name is Maddy and she was the inspiration for my first PEAS book, **Eat Your Peas for Young Adults**. At the very beginning of her book I made a place to write in my phone number so she knew I was serious about being available. And right beside the phone number I put my promise to listen—really listen—whenever that call came.

Soon after the book was published, people began to ask me if I had the same promise and affirmation for adults. I realized it isn't just young people who need to be reminded how truly special they are. We all do.

Today Maddy is thriving and giving hope to others in her life.
If someone has given you this book, you must be a pretty amazing person and they wanted to let you know it. If you purchased Eat Your Peas for Me for yourself, hooray! you already know you are special! Take it to heart.
Believe it, and remind yourself often.

Wishing you peas and plenty of joy,

Cheryl Karpen

P.S. If you are wondering why I named the collection, Eat Your Peas...it's my way of saying, "Stay healthy. I love and cherish you. I want you to live **forever**!"

A portion of the profits from the
Eat Your Peas Collection
will benefit empowerment programs
for youth and adults.

A special note from the author

I realized not long ago
that if you *think* you are only a small pea in the pod,
you will remain a small pea in the pod.

I believe each and every one of us
is destined for greatness.

We only need to open our eyes and see the
truth and beauty inside of us.
Sometimes we simply need a nudge to
see what's been there all along.

That's why I wrote this book.

It's for all of us who have ever
doubted our own magnificence or forgotten
how to take a loving look in the mirror.

I wish I could meet each one
of you and tell you how truly amazing you are.

I believe in you.

— Cheryl

About the author

"Eat Your Peas"

A self-proclaimed dreamer, Cheryl
spends her time imagining and creating
between the historic river town of Anoka, Minnesota
and the seaside village of Islamorada, Florida.

An effervescent speaker, Cheryl brings inspiration,
insight, and humor to corporations,
professional organizations and churches.
Learn more about her at: www.cherylkarpen.com

About the illustrator

Sandy Fougner artfully weaves
a love for design, illustration and
interiors with being a wife
and mother of three sons.

The Eat Your Peas Collection™

Takes only 3-minutes to read but you'll want to hold on to it forever!

Eat Your Peas for Someone Special
Eat Your Peas for Girlfriends
Eat Your Peas for Daughters
Eat Your Peas for Sons
Eat Your Peas for Mothers
Eat Your Peas for Sisters
Eat Your Peas for New Moms
Eat Your Peas for Grandkids
Eat Your Peas for Teens
Eat Your Peas for Gardening Friends

New titles are SPROUTING up all the time!

Heart and Soul Collection

To Let You Know I Care
Hope for a Hurting Heart
Can We Try Again? Finding a way back to love

To view a complete collection, visit us on-line at www.eatyourpeas.com

Eat Your Peas™ for Me

For more information or to locate a store near you contact:

Gently Spoken Communications
P.O. Box 245
Anoka, Minnesota 55303
1-877-224-7886
www.gentlyspoken.com